A NEW CURE FOR INSOMNIA
Copyright © Ian Passey 2023

All Rights Reserved

ISBN 978-1-3999-6939-0

First Published 2023 by
Cynical Thrills Books

A NEW CURE FOR INSOMNIA

the
humdrum
express

To

Dickie Round

All the best,

Ian Paisley

X

Thanks to:

Steve Lamacq, Mick Lown, Andrew Boswell, Carl Bayliss,
Chris Taylor-Ashcroft, Ted Cartwright, Rich Payne,
Curtis Fudge, Brendan Moran, Nick J Townsend, Dom Dunlea,
Tracy and Arthur

Finally, to every single person who has bought a record, CD,
book, T-shirt, mug or a pair of Humdrum Y-fronts; to those
lovely people who have appeared in a video, attended a gig,
promoted a show, downloaded a song or even just listened
to a stream (that 0.003 pence is very much appreciated!)

Thank you all so much xxx

Ian Passey 2023

Contents:

7th October, 2009

It was the first chilly night of autumn and I was aboard
the 19:10 out of Kidderminster.
My destination was Nicole's Bar in Birmingham's Jewellery
Quarter where, on Wednesdays, they hosted The Secret Music
Club.

"I hope it's not too much of a secret," I thought to myself, as the
train rattled its way through the long tunnel between Old Hill
and Rowley Regis.

This is how the event had been described on Myspace (Hi Tom!)

**"The Secret Music Club happens every Wednesday night at
Nicole's, 18 Hall Street, Birmingham.**

* The best local and touring acts
* Great beer at recession-busting prices
* Silent movie backdrops
* Open mic session for poets and musicians (ALL welcome!)
* Great vibes!
* Free Entry
*** A favourite of many touring musicians, this is perhaps
the best little gig in Britain..!"**

Well, it sounded perfect. The sort of night that my
blossoming/late blooming talent deserved...

I was there pretty early, around eight o'clock.
The promoter, Mike, was setting up the modest P.A. ready for
the evening's entertainment.
There would be an open mic session to begin with followed
by this week's special guest artist. They were obviously stuck
for a major touring act as they'd asked me to do it!

The deal was a forty minute set with a pint glass passed around as a thank you; the words 'pay' and 'day' couldn't help but spring to mind.

I'd exchanged pleasantries with Mike before ordering myself a "recession busting" Guinness (at usual pub price) and taking a seat. I was the first one there, unfashionably early.

There was a big screen behind the stage area showing tonight's Masterchef, which was then followed by a Charlie Chaplin film. I half watched it, occasionally turning round to the window behind, in anticipation of the arrival of music-loving masses.

Thirty minutes later and I'd finished nursing my drink.
The place was still empty and the film was losing its appeal.
I was, by now, feeling uneasy.
I got up from my seat and viewed the street outside.
Not even a passing car, let alone throngs of excited entertainment enthusiasts.

Mike had disappeared to the bar next door.
We'd long since exhausted small talk pleasantries and there wasn't really much else for either of us to say.

I ordered another pint and a bag of crisps.
Ninety minutes later and we were still the only two people there.

"Do you want to play your set?" Mike asked.

"Not really."

I picked up my guitar case, nodded in his direction and headed for the door.

Double Edged Swords

A new cure for insomnia that's more than just a myth
Audio books by former Arsenal striker Alan Smith
The chill out zone, meets nasal monotone

Fashion advice from eBay sellers, I can't help but doubt
So many items claim, "Look great with jeans on a night out"
Can't get to grips, with these style tips

I have to wonder if there'll ever be a time
When bands stop posting rehearsal clips online
You may be rock 'n' roll saviours
But they do you no favours

The local kids swimming club pack shopping at a cost
I leave the supermarket with my bread and crisps all squashed
They should be briefed, put tins underneath

My zest for the high life, it seems, has ebbed away
As I struggle with a word search on a rainy holiday
Dark feelings lurk, knowing I'm soon back at work

Monday morning daydreams as a colleague reminisces
Detailed descriptions of Sunday league misses

Just when you think things may be going your way
You realise you can't win
It's like being offered a slot on 'Later with Jools'
As long as you let him join in
Boogie-woogie piano chords, double edged swords

I can't help but feel ungrateful for gestures from the smug
Who take pity on my plight by sending me a cyber-hug
They all should fear my cyber clip round the ear

People think I'm stubborn and it's getting out of hand
But they don't realise I've got a mate in a tribute band
Though not condoned, he's not yet been disowned

I'm not always against an idle preconception
Never trust a man who owns the Chubby Brown collection

Just when you think things may be going your way
You realise you can't win
It's like being offered a slot on 'Later with Jools'
As long as you let him join in
Boogie-woogie piano chords, double edged swords

Given that the first line has provided this book with its title, it seems fitting to start with Double Edged Swords.

My most aired song on BBC 6 Music, its release in 2015 was accompanied by a promotional video, the first of many rewarding visual collaborations with renowned musician and film maker, Nick J. Townsend.

It starred, as is often the case in Humdrum videos, Mr. Andrew Boswell - the man of 1000 faces (all of them the same!)

The opening scene, an obvious nod to Subterranean Homesick Blues, was ambitiously done in one take.
I had to catch a train from Cradley Heath, with cue cards in hand, to get off at Stourbridge Junction where the camera would be rolling.

A slight hitch meant I had to go back to film it again, but as we pulled in for the second time it soon became clear we'd need a third attempt.
The train took a slight detour, coming to a halt on the opposite platform!

A few weeks after its release, someone posted the video on Twitter and tagged Alan Smith in it.
His very sporting response was,
"Not exactly what I'd call complimentary, but I'll take it."

If there's ever any sort of demand for an audio version of this book, I know who I'm going to ask.
If he declines, or proves to be too expensive, I'll read it myself in his voice!

It's Nearly Time (To Ditch My Old Friends)

It's nearly time to ditch my old friends; it's what my agent
recommends
Don't be offended, there's no harm intended
It would be nice if things could always stay the same
But I'm meandering to fame
And you're a bind; I don't mean to be unkind

I know we'll say that 'we'll keep in touch' and 'oh yes, we must'
But once I've got the break I've been waiting for
You won't see me for dust

It's nearly time to ditch my old friends; it's what my label
recommends
Don't be offended, there's no harm intended
I'm going to be one of the faces
Hang around in higher places
Goodbye to chav hats, hello to cravats

I need to be with movers and shakers, people just like me
But I ain't going to find them in the pub so I'm off to a gallery

It's nearly time to ditch my old friends; it's what my ego
recommends
Been making plans to get the whole world in my hands
Did I tell you that I'm going to be
One of those stars that works for charity
I know I said they bore me, but it might help the public adore me

I don't mean to blow my own trumpet but guess what I've just
seen
I've been described as 'thinking woman's crumpet' in OK
Magazine

Now it's two years later and I think I've made it, dig this if you can
I've had a call from a celebrity cricket team who have asked me to
be 12th man

I think it's time for me to ring my old mates; it's what my good
news dictates
Me? Big headed? No way! I just thought that I'd make your day
But as I call I am surprised
Told the number's not been recognised
Perhaps you changed it a while ago and forgot to let my agent
know

Two very early
Humdrum Express
promo shots.

Inspired by
Tony Hancock,
trying to look
clever by holding
a Bertrand Russell
book!

Both photos
2007

Game, Set and Match (Fixing)

He's off to play tennis, practice his backhand
Got a huge sports bag and a new headband
Barley water fuels his expertise
White shirts, tight shorts - NEW BALLS PLEASE!

With fellow club members, spends his time
Either down at the net or on the baseline
Some are highly strung, just like his racket
But he's amongst friends, shared income bracket

Said there'd be fewer confrontations
If club rules were used in off-court situations
There'd be less disagreement and moments of regret
If arguments were settled by playing a let

There's nothing quite like a sunny afternoon
Down at Wimbers at the end of June
The one time of year he can be upfront
About the fact he pays to hear girls grunt

An SW19 love affair
When he's back home, pretends he's still there
From his youth in the garden, pretending he's Bjorn
To clapping when a pigeon lands on his lawn

As British hopes plummet and the rain begins
Get strawberries in a punnet and a jug of iced Pimm's
Raise a glass - Bottoms up! Down the hatch!
To serve! To volley! To game, set and match!

The Gig Chatterer

Home from work, I put my best shirt on
I'm out tonight, catching up with friends
Meet early for a few drinks, and then onto a gig
The perfect start to my weekend

Acoustic bands are best, less need for me to shout
My naturally booming speaking voice will do
I'm 6'4" and I quite like to stand near the front
Helps me get a better view

I'm socialising, why the hell should I be apologising?
I've paid my way in

We've finally got served and I'm holding court
Just my luck the first act's about to play
I'm going to tell you about my ailments
And what happened to me at work today

I'm socialising, why the hell should I be apologising?
I've paid my way in

I've been called disrespectful by the easily upset
Who asked why can't I just enjoy the show?
It's not as if I even know this track
I'll sing along when they play one I know

I'm socialising, why the hell should I be apologising?
I thought speech was free?
The king of gig chatter, I don't take in subject matter

Or hear this song's about me

The scourge of performers and gig-goers alike, chatterers are, infuriatingly, becoming the norm at live events.

I'll leave the rest of the page blank, so you can write in your own swear words to describe these ignorant, inconsiderate, self-important morons...

Motivational Wall Art

Coffee and cake culture, new vape flavours
Waistcoat Wednesday, competitive savers
Black Friday, white noise
Ignoring Blue Planet, watching Mrs Brown's Boys

Sales are booming of motivational wall art

The gift of the gab, no listening attribute
Practising a power stance in a Teflon suit
The mediocre with mass YouTube subscribers
What's for tea? Microwaved micro fibres

Sales are booming of motivational wall art

Transfer deadline failings fuel abusive chants
Resting on laurels, tending hardy plants
We're all innocent till rumours are rife
And the views of singers I once liked say nothing to me
about my life

Political U-turns, a tactical false nine
Trends for big eyebrows will be frowned upon in time
Diverting tactics, feigning surprise
Ultracrepidarians are on the rise

Sales are booming of motivational wall art

Under false impressions, we're unnerved
Another minute's silence impeccably observed
A celebratory tattoo so it won't be forgotten
The battle of the egos, from the top to the bottom

Gig goers watch through hand held devices
Can't afford a drink at sponsored venue prices
Uneven paving, irate shoppers
Night club toilet selfies, patriotic litter droppers
Coming in to bowl the spin master's misinforming
That an ice bucket challenge could help end global warming
Cigars for fast food chain tycoons
Golden handshakes for silver spoons
The ref's looked at his watch, full time's closing in
Got two single use razors for his double chin
Low expectations in high demand
Polluted beaches, heads in the sand

Sales are booming of motivational wall art

I'm as guilty as the next man when it comes to focusing on trivial matters and sometimes ignoring the more important issues, but I can honestly say I've never been tempted to purchase a 'Shine Bright like a Diamond' canvass from Wilko!

Accompanied by another Nick J Townsend video, Motivational Wall Art was set in a school, with teachers played by kids and the adults being taught a lesson on the environmental shit-show they've left them to deal with.

A year in the planning (these things aren't just thrown together, you know) we were very kindly given permission to use Offmore Primary School as our location.

Ahead of that, Andrew Boswell had, once again, demonstrated his acting versatility by tidying up the streets of Kidderminster as part of the film that would be shown in class to our students. Not all superheroes wear Hi-Viz, but this one certainly does!

It's worth pointing out that disposable plastic coffee cup lids were easily the most dropped items in our town centre.

Coffee and cake culture, indeed...

Brave Boy

I'm not alone in suffering from needle phobia
It's both frightening and hard to justify
The thought of getting a small reward
Sometimes helps me through it
Seemingly, they're in short supply

I got a brave boy sticker, but I was hoping for an enamel badge
I got a brave boy sticker, but I was hoping for an enamel badge

I'm aware that the cost of a badge might be seen
As a drain on resources
But this jab was an achievement for me
It wasn't me who spent 37 billion
On a failed track and trace system
And millions more on deficient PPE

I got a brave boy sticker, but I was hoping for an enamel badge
I got a brave boy sticker, but I was hoping for an enamel badge

Amazing NHS staff alleviated
The nervousness I couldn't help displaying
My fears, so patiently tolerated
Their endurance skills honed observing claps in lieu of paying

For 24 hours after my vaccination
My temperature rose, and I felt sick
Those daily Downing Street briefings
Left me similarly nauseous
Also brought about by a small prick

I got a brave boy sticker, but I was hoping for an enamel badge
I got a brave boy sticker, but I was hoping for an enamel badge
I got a brave boy sticker, but I was hoping
And like health workers, I'm left hoping...

*An "anthem" for fellow trypanophobia sufferers, this is the tale of
my first Covid jab.*

Back In The Day

I recently came 4th on a reality show; it's time to reveal my plans
I'm getting the band back together, as a special thanks to the fans
We never made any money back then, but what people tend to forget
Is we were young, having fun and no-one explained
The difference between gross and net

Tickets go on sale in the morning; we'd really love to see you there
It's going to be just like the old days, though without the shoulder pads and hair
On the school run I've pondered my life change, more family than front man
I got by as the face of Toilet Duck - ignoring jibes about careers down the pan

Not quite the original line up - Which I know, for some, is a shame
But Terry's no longer with us, couldn't handle life without minor fame
Paul and Gaz are back on board, though I've heard that Brian's miffed
But the promise of a payday and the passing of time couldn't heal our old rift

Adored by the ladies, back then it was all on a plate
It's cruel to say I'm stuck in the 80's, but they're the times I'd love to re-create
Reminiscing in our tour bus, about travelling in a clapped out van
It used to be lock up your daughters, we joke it's now more lock up your Nan

Name checked by cool new bands, I hope it helps to end the
Royalties drought
Seems everyone else is re-forming, it's only fair that we don't miss
out
Be careful not to pastiche yourselves, I heard our old rivals say
Shame they never took their own advice... Back in the day

The press reported gigs as half empty, though that wasn't quite
the case
Ask any of the handful of diehards, they'll tell you we rocked the
place
Promoters were slightly ambitious, arenas perhaps too big
I was the only bloke in the venue not wearing a mullet wig

So now the tour is over and I'm left to face my fears
I used to dream of a comeback, in what the papers call my
wilderness years
Time to face the music, hope it's not the end of the line
The new songs were met with indifference, they just need to be
given time

I need something to swell the coffers, but we'll have to wait and
see
Who is first to come up with an offer...

Perhaps a music channel or talent show panel
My pension plan needs a tour of Japan
New recording sessions or I could take acting lessons
I'm sure I could cope with a panto or soap
Or failing that...

It's back to reality

Martin Kemp....

He's handsome, overconfident, cheesy and smug.
Frankly, I can't stand the bloke!
Let's not airbrush those ScS furniture adverts from his career - they're
probably the best thing he's ever done!

Back In The Day was originally inspired by his appearance on
'I'm a Celebrity... Get Me Out of Here.'

Around the same time, OMD were sailing on the seven seas of another
comeback and I was unfortunate enough to hear a radio interview with
Andy McCluskey.

It may have been a one-off, but he seemed a bit full of himself in a Kemp
kind of way.

I certainly don't need any encouragement to lump all 80's pop stars into
the same needy, self-important basket!

Give It A Whirl

On November 13th, 1986
A man was killed during his first rehearsal, for a live TV stunt
Called "Hang 'Em High" it involved bungee jumping
From an exploding box suspended from a crane

The attaching rope sprang loose from its eyebolt during the jump
Instantly, Michael Lush died
Future shows were scrapped two days later
And ringmaster, Noel Edmonds, resigned

The inquest recorded a verdict of misadventure
The jury were informed of neglect

It was revealed that the weight of a bag of sugar could have been
opened the clip
Out of twenty demonstrations it sprang loose fourteen times
No safety officer on hand, no way for Lush to contact the ground
And no-one with him in case he changed his mind

The man who died in the name of viewing figures
Nervously delayed his final fall
Some peoples lives are filled with second chances
Others given no chance at all

The inquest recorded a verdict of misadventure
The jury were informed of neglect

I can't stand Noel Edmonds...
(There appears to be a theme developing here!)

The tragic tale of Michael Lush came up in conversation one night, so I
did a bit of research to assist my vague recollections of the sad story.

I have to admit to stealing a few of the lines straight from Wikipedia.
I didn't think anyone would notice and I probably would have got away
with it, if it wasn't for those pesky kids!

Edmonds got away with it though.
He always does.

Nozstock
2017

Castle & Falcon
Birmingham
29/10/2021
supporting
CUD

Botox Lunch Break

Got a wire wool brush to remove hard skin
And a recipe book called eat yourself thin
There's no rule to losing weight, it says
So I'm digesting a page each day

Got a tip from a Sunday magazine
Rub legs with sunflower margarine
Then place cucumber over eyes
Guaranteed to attract the flies

I'm on a mental and physical quest
To reverse the ageing process

Sun beds make your skin look old
So every week I get mine sprayed gold
Giving off a glow through the salon door
Here comes Pantone 164
Exfoliating facial scrub
Rejuvenating in the hot tub
Pleasure meets pain, while relaxing
I'm booked in for an intimate waxing

On a mental and physical quest
To reverse the ageing process

Afternoon's spent traipsing round stores
Trying to find a coat just like yours

Carrot juice sipped on a spa weekend
Cabbage soup diet, lost all my friends
Bottled water, slim-fast shake
Salsa-cise, botox lunch break
Medical science has invented a cream
To help boost flagging self esteem...
Demand is great, the price even higher
I'm so glad it's something I don't require

On a mental and physical quest
To reverse the ageing process

Festival at Home

Got a bucket hat, wellies on and sunscreen applied
Though I know this weekend, I won't venture outside
My friends have all gone and left me on my own
I couldn't get a ticket, so I'm festivalling at home...

Got cheap cans of cider, scattered on the floor
And, although I'm not quite sad enough to pitch a tent indoors
I've been studying the line up to see who's on, when and where
And I hope that watching on TV's as good as being there

For those in attendance, there's a price to be paid
Low battery catastrophe for the "I was there" brigade
In a field of thousands, I'd feel alone
When the crowd all sing that song that was used to sell iphones

There's a grumble in the wine tent, where service seems slow
The glamper's stocks of ice are worryingly low
They'll voice their disapproval at the hospitality
Later on that evening from their five star tepee

Of course, the TV coverage fails to come close
It's all described as wonderful and I think I've overdosed
There's no sign of the bands that I'd have enjoyed
But a full set on the red button from the ones that I'd avoid

I know it's cruel to raise a smile as I watch the pouring rain
And the wind blows the sound to a town eight miles away
But pretty soon, a payback for my pettiness will come
When I try avoiding crashing bores who've left their wristbands on

Festival at Home was the first song I ever had played by Steve Lamacq on his 6 Music drive time show.
I was working alongside my good friend Dom Dunlea, listening to 6 as we always did whilst screen printing our lives away...

"Coming up on today's show, we've got all the usual gubbins. We've got music from the likes of The Pixies, PJ Harvey, Suede, The Jam...
Lots of new stuff too, including an interesting single from The Humdrum Express, which might be of interest to those of you going to a certain festival over the next few days."

We looked at each other in disbelief! An absolute thrill!

Lammo played it three times that week, the run up to Glastonbury.

I'd written the song following the previous year's Worthy Farm festival, when the BBC had really started to ramp up their coverage and promotion of the event.

We'd had a full week of build up and I remember feeling disappointed on the Friday evening as I tuned in to watch the TV coverage. (This was before the multi Red Button options of today).

A mate of mine, Ade Bailey, was hilariously scathing on social media which gave further encouragement that a song on the subject might strike a chord with others.

Christmas with Evan Dando

I know this may sound like an unlikely tale, but
I once spent Christmas Day on Bondi Beach with Evan Dando

Exploring the southern hemisphere can throw up so many new
experiences and unlikely situations
None more so than the sight of the 90's slacker pin-up casually
wandering amongst jubilant festive revellers
The temperature was close to 30 degrees, but Evan wore a
sweatshirt, jeans and cowboy boots which further enhanced his
cool guy reputation
I, meanwhile, looked every inch the weediest bloke ever to
set foot on an Aussie shoreline.

I know this may sound like an unlikely tale, but
I once spent Christmas Day on Bondi Beach with Evan Dando

As luck would have it, upon my arrival in Sydney, I'd purchased
a cheap guitar which I'd happened to take with me to the beach
I must add here though, that I've never been that guy who takes
an acoustic to a festival for late night noodling.
Why do they do that?
Do they blindly hope to be discovered or seriously think nearby
campers enjoy their repertoire of Oasis covers?
Anyway, back to the story.
My mates and I somehow ended up joining Evan and his friends
Where we were treated to a set of Lemonheads' classics

I know this may sound like an unlikely tale, but
I once spent Christmas Day on Bondi Beach with Evan Dando

I remember Evan telling me he'd come to the beach to get over
the disappointment of a Santa no-show due to transportation
problems
A combination of star-struck nerves and strong drink led me to
make an idiotic joke about it being a "shame about sleigh"
I felt such a fool but he kindly handed the guitar back to me
Asking if I'd like to play something
Well, I'd recently been busking 'Into Your Arms' so we performed
a duet
One of THEE classic moments in Rock n Roll history!

I know this may sound like an unlikely tale, but
I once spent Christmas Day on Bondi Beach with Evan Dando

I acknowledge a slight exaggeration over the years, but it's
probably no surprise that this has since become one of my
favourite anecdotes, repeated on an almost weekly basis to the
deftly disguised delight of work mates.
Whilst Evan and I admit, "We've never been too good with names"
That Bondi Bond remains so strong that if either of us happened
to be in trouble we'd pick up the phone and the other would drop
everything
To, once again, become a bit part in each others lives

I know this may sound like an unlikely tale, but
I once spent Christmas Day on Bondi Beach with Evan Dando

Talking of my mate Dom Dunlea, this one was inspired by him!

Working side by side for 20 years, he was my Humdrum sounding board.

Every song idea, gig plan and live performance anecdote was shared with him on a daily basis.

Dom's a top quality stencil artist, better known as 'Deeds' in the art world.

In return for listening to my exciting plans, he regularly bored me to tears with his tales of spray cans and paint jams….. (Love you, Deedsy!)

Christmas with Evan Dando is actually a true story; I'd met "Ev" (he loved me calling him that!) on Bondi Beach when I spent a year in Australia in the 1990's.

Every single time The Lemonheads were played on the radio while we were working, I'd remind Dom of my classic story.

I don't think he ever got tired of hearing it….

I'm no oil painting...

... but I am, at least, the subject of this quality piece of stencil art from Dom "Deeds" Dunlea!

Novelty Tie

I swapped cigarette packs that said, "Smoking kills"
For ones that warned, "Might reduce fitness"
I view housework as a spectator sport...
I'm a Je-Hoover's witness
I'm aware my somewhat laid back approach
Is often much maligned
I'd chase the materialistic dream
But I've got too much on my mind

At least I'm not denying
The fact that life's passing me by
You said you'd tear down the system from within
Now you're wearing a novelty tie

Dining in on own brand cup-a-soup
Displays thriftiness hard to refuse
It's a means to an end; I'm saving up for a camera
Like the ones estate agents use
Baby boomers devoid of humour
Try to shift the blame for their mistakes
While Brexiteer bruisers in backstreet boozers
Bemoan the price of Benidorm breaks

At least I'm not denying
The fact that life's passing me by
You said you'd tear down the system from within
Now you're wearing a novelty tie

I don't dwell on the years that I won't get back
I still hope to get back on track
I've applied for a job as the bloke who names
Tribute bands and hurricanes

It's not just men who are guilty
Ageing is no gender divider
One day you're a young Debbie Harry
The next more like Dee Snider
I don't mean to be shallow
The importance placed on looks is absurd
Although I fear ending up as one of those blokes
Who resemble a fledgling bird

At least I'm not denying
The fact that life's passing me by
You said you'd tear down the system from within
Now you're wearing a novelty tie

Clone Town Blues
artwork by
Deeds

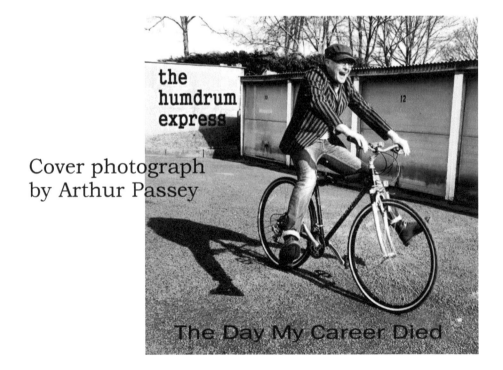

Cover photograph
by Arthur Passey

Clone Town Blues

Misguided information, misleading get-out clause
Requests and frustrations, misspelt on subway walls
Ignored all the warnings, failed to heed the news
I woke up this morning with a bout of clone town blues

Chain stores and petrol prices
Save me the time
I can't afford to visit your town
But it's probably just the same as mine

Sponsored imposition, beware the outstretched hand
A no-win competition, to sell out to a global brand
Passer by friction, fashion sense despair
Unexplained addiction to loose fit leisurewear

Chain stores and petrol prices
Save me the time
I can't afford to visit your town
But it's probably just the same as mine

Weekly Monday morning hating
Freedom bid farewell
Down beat on street corners, waiting
Sandwiches in hand, for lifts to hell

A radio phone-in, I was just about to ring
Halt live debate on cloning with an ad for Burger King
Too late to call in favours, escape remains unplayed
Narked by nosy neighbours and the "been there, done that"
brigade

Chain stores and petrol prices
Save me the time
I can't afford to visit your town
But it's probably just the same as mine

I bet there aren't many music producers to have invented a unique sound called The Genital Screech!

The first three Humdrum Express albums (All Aboard, Little Victories and Elevation of Trivia) were self produced.
I had no previous experience but really enjoyed the process of building up the songs and adding different layers with LOTS of effects!
I listened back to those recordings as part of my research for this book.
I think the best word to describe my thoughts would be... unimpressed!

The fourth album, Clone Town Blues, was the start of an ongoing, fruitful collaboration with esteemed producer and inventor of the genital screech, Mick Lown. It's fair to say that I would never have had the same sort of recognition and national airplay without his expertise and ability to help bring the songs to life.

Like all great partnerships, we met in the pub. We've somehow since managed to combine drinking and recording sessions, going on to produce the albums The Day My Career Died, Ultracrepidarian Soup and Forward Defensive, along with the stand-alone Lookalike Bond EP.

I was going to tell the tale of how we once found a pair of tights in the studio and wrapped them around the neck of the guitar to create a subtle dampening sound.

Then I remembered Mick was still wearing them, so thought better of it!

Ultracrepidarian Soup cover photo
by Arthur Passey

Cryptic Self Pity

Five to three, Saturday afternoon
Let me entertain you blares out through the stadium tannoy
speakers
As a Tony Pulis side run out, hell bent on nullifying the
opposition
Before, no doubt, sneaking an undeserved late winner
About as much fun as a soon to become former friend
Who tells you he's not only going to keep his Movember
But also plans to cultivate a hipster beard
It can only add to the uneasiness already created
By him wearing brogues with no socks

Aspiring celebrities take to twitter
Following the tragic news of the passing of a D-lister
They once spoke to at a party in 2010
RIP with exclamation marks
PR condolences, united in false emotion
Lives touched, shaped and inspired by what was, in truth
An unmemorable conversation
Time to reassess lifetime goals as a tribute
All that she wants is another baby, a commemorative tattoo
And a blue tick

Going for a pint has never been so competitive
Bragging rights secured by the highest percentage and highest
price
I'm talking, of course, about the modern day horror
That is pubs serving drinks in branded glasses
Smug high fives in the marketing department
While customers complain to bar staff
About the use of inferior trademarks on busy nights
I'm still at a loss as to why eating and drinking
Are now described as cheeky
When I'd stupidly assumed they were basic human needs

Coming up... a tired old band
Set to announce they're either branching out or going back to
their roots
By doing an arboretum tour
Spotted in the small ads...
Graphologist seeks calligrapher
I think the writing's on the wall
Voluntary work's OK for those that can afford it
While recreational cycling appears far to popular these days
I once wrote an open letter on these and other subjects to
Channel 4
Sadly, out of habit, I sealed the envelope before posting

To be avoided:
Those who combine a kagoul and clip board
Psychic meeting attendees who wrongly predict
You'd be interested in their evening
And anyone of the opinion that Harry Redknapp
Should have been made England manager
Teenagers who listen to the likes of
Hall & Oats, Phil Collins and Dire Straits
With a hint of irony
Teenagers who listen to the likes of
Hall & Oats, Phil Collins and Dire Straits
Without a hint of irony

I'm going home to post cryptic self pity

Still on a high from the Festival at Home airplay on 6 Music, I knew I'd quickly have to come up with another single in a bid to strike while the iron was warm!

It was written, almost entirely, on an old Yamaha QY70 sequencer with a spoken lyric and Mick's added distorted 'hooligan' guitar sound!

On the day I was due to record the vocals, the news broke that Tony Pulis had left his role as manager of Crystal Palace.
I was pretty sure he'd land another job ahead of the Cryptic Self Pity release, but didn't for one minute think he'd rock up at my team, West Bromwich Albion, where his dire brand of football almost crushed my lifelong love of the game.

45

Speed Awareness Course

33 in a 30, on an open road, downhill
More lack of concentration than acceleration thrill
Round the corner, captured, by a hand-held device
My chances 50/50 at best, if the reading was precise

My worst fears confirmed by a fund-raising calculator
The dreaded, headed papers arrived three mornings later
Must face an ordeal for my careless free-wheel, so I'm logged on
in my front room
For a speed awareness course, ironically via Zoom!

Uneasy introductions precede reminders of restrictions
Our consultant conducts conversation on car connected
convictions
Positive vibes are welcomed, interaction viewed essential
And anything mentioned throughout the course is strictly
confidential

Stopping distances debated, the Highway Code embraced
It'll be some distance until we stop as discussions are pedestrian
paced
Sally, in Salisbury, struggles with sporadic, slow connection
While Mike, who I already dislike, answers every bloody question!

We're informed that calmness is vital to help aid speed adherence
So I calmly ask if pot-hole cameras might, one day, make an
appearance
Mike plays U2 albums, to help relax on a journey's duration
I give him a driver's hand signal, road-rage gesticulation!

Three long hours, with strangers, connected by a screen
Driven by the chance to keep our driving license clean
If you ever exceed the limit, I'd exceedingly endorse
Accepting the fine, taking the points and speedily swerving the
course

John Otway

Chas 'n' Dave

Staying Inn

He's built a home bar in the garden, at great expense
To get on up on his neighbour on the other side of the fence
His own Club Tropicana, where the drinks are free
Got a plaque above the entrance with his name as licensee

Cul-de-sac harmony's wearing thin
Since the opening of The Staying Inn

He's built a home bar in the garden, where lock-ins are always allowed
Generous measures served up for a small, exclusive crowd
For those without an invite, there's a virtual tour online
To view ostentatious optics and his subtle neon sign

Cul-de-sac harmony's wearing thin
Since the opening of The Staying Inn

He's built a home bar in the garden, Las Vegas themed
Elvis karaoke, Sky Sports, bar snacks, big screen
Rings a bell to call last orders which helps keep him amused
He's got six bespoke barstools, though five are rarely used

Dedicated to those people who not only built pubs in their gardens during lockdown, but also made sure EVERYBODY knew about it!

Manscape Monday

My hobbies include my wardrobe and my hair
My fitness routine and my daily skincare
I hope my chosen fragrance adds to my allure
Along with my frequently scheduled manicure

I regularly keep downstairs untidiness at bay
It's just another Manscape Monday

A fashion sense fuelled by fear of someone wearing the same
Stretch nylon fabric compliments my well-toned frame
A fresh ensemble each day, to suit the weather
With trade-mark unexpected colours worn together

A monthly accumulation of designer bags
A dedicated follower of price tags

Got a new set of teeth
To add to my disguise
But like my heroes on TV
I could have done with a smaller size

Of course, there are those who choose to mock my chic finess
With small-minded opinions on how I like to dress
From shouts in the street, to harsh online pot shots
Ridiculed for trying to make the best of what I've got

While others vocal views only highlight what they lack
I pretend its water off a peacock's back

Manscape Monday
Wish it was Sunday
That's my fun day
My marathon run day

End of Part One

We got cars, once driven forever smitten
Toilet rolls, as soft as a kitten
Hands that do dishes feel as soft as your face
Believe that and you must be a fruit and nut case
Get busy with the fizzy – soda stream.
Just one Cornetto from Wall's ice cream
A drink's too wet without Rich Tea
All the milky bars are on me!

But non chocoholics won't understand
They should melt in your mouth and not in your hand
I like aero bubbles and a mars a day
But I know the lady loves Milk Tray
Made with a glass and a half of milk
Why have cotton when you can have silk?
Milky Way won't spoil appetites
I'm trying to give 'em up but it's one of those nights

You want Eastern promise? Get a Turkish delight
A Topic for a hazelnut in every bite
Blue Ribband Blues; Work, rest and play
Re-record not fade away
He's splashed it all over - You can't half smell him
The mark of a man - If you see Sid, tell him
Hai Karate, Insignia, Old Spice, Lynx
The man that doesn't have to try too hard stinks

Snap crackle pop, sugar puffs, bran flakes
Exceedingly good Mr Kipling cakes
Your flexible friend..? I was denied access
To the listening bank that likes to say yes
So is she or isn't she? Harmony hair
You want weak lager? Follow the bear
Is it live or is it Memorex?
Poor old Malcolm's forgot his Sinex

This, we're told, is the age of the train
We're getting there, we'll take the strain
If you go by car, take my advice
Clunk click. Think once, think twice
Sometimes you do and sometimes you brew
Tetley, PG Tips, Typhoo
Shredded wheat, I bet you can't eat three
You'll have to wait and see

Mr Muscle loves the jobs you hate
No fillings today mum – Colgate!
She flies like a bird on nimble bread
Domestos kills all known germs dead
Get a Peugeot, for the drive of your life
You'll never put a better bit of butter on your knife
A million housewives every day
Shout Accrington Stanley, who are they?

It's a lot less bovver when you cut the grass
Harp stays sharp 'til the bottom of the glass
Beanz meanz Heinz, the longer lasting snack
JR Hartley put the freshness back
Now I'm all confused, can't sleep at night
My brain's like smash and me ears are alight
But since I gave up television it's all become clear
It's only a commercial, CALM DOWN DEAR!

I often get a headache, trying to remember all the words to this one.
A tense, nervous headache...

Blue Plaque Building

I reversed into a blue plaque building
Escaped with a clean bill of health
Blamed it on my night-blindness
And clutter on the parcel shelf

Always try...
To give the impression of owning a car with fully working air
conditioning by driving on the hottest days of summer with the
windows closed
It can also dramatically aid weight loss, although only in
conjunction with a calorie controlled diet
Channel five; it's been weeks since I sent my suggestion for a TV
show where all four members of New Order try to last longest
without mentioning band finances
The loser to endure an evening with Tony Hadley and the Kemp
brothers which could then, of course, be filmed for a future series.

I reversed into a blue plaque building
Escaped with a clean bill of health
Blamed it on my night-blindness
And clutter on the parcel shelf

I'm out on...
A crawl of pubs I never go in, merely to confirm suspicions and, it
would appear, I've walked in on a Peaky Blinders theme night
It's true! There really are adults who describe food as yummy and
say,
"Hey! Can I get?" when ordering sour shots
The type, I'm sure, to post regular updates from fitness apps and
progress on flat pack furniture building
Their love of street food, Bon Iver, male Ugg boots, wattle and
daub
And the fact they hilariously watch cookery shows... on ketchup
TV

I reversed into a blue plaque building
Escaped with a clean bill of health
Blamed it on my night-blindness
And clutter on the parcel shelf

The sun's hot...
And the drinks, ice cold
But here comes a bloke in shorts and flip flops with a ukulele,
promising a set of quirky covers and earnest originals.
Surely the time has come for someone to invent...
THE REMOTE CONTROL WASP!
It could also be used to distract opposition goalkeepers during
penalty shoot-outs

I reversed into a blue plaque building
Escaped with a clean bill of health
Blamed it on my night-blindness
And clutter on the parcel shelf

HEY! Can I get a round of sour shots?

Plaque Day
(Memories of the Market Tavern)

A return of familiar faces, slightly longer in the tooth
Assembled for the confirmation of a well spent youth
Let's reunite on Plaque Day, to unveil the souvenir
And remember hazy 90's nights and friends no longer here
Our very own CBGB's

I saw Funbug, Scumbug, Polarbug, Cake and The Pale Kings
But kick myself daily, for missing The Senseless Things
Cows in the corridor, the windows were jammed
The toilets weren't healthy, we didn't give a damn
As long as we didn't breathe in

Some of the bands explored the sights while they were
passing through
Lou Barlow in Fair Discount is a rumour I hope's true

Bikers in the front bar, farmers out the back
Indie kids, in between, in fear of an attack
Though the only confrontation that I've never forgotten
Is someone trying to pull the head off Frank Sidebottom
You know they did
They really did!

A makeshift stage and barriers when Carter came to town
They could have done with a makeshift drummer when the tape
machine broke down

Raise a pint of snakebite to the promoter of the bands
Who fly posted the subways and, on gig nights, stamped the hands
Of the incoming grebos, the crusties and the goths
The only Kiddy boy to book Redd Kross
From Badge nights to Plaque Days

A return of familiar faces, slightly longer in the tooth
Assembled for the confirmation of a well spent youth
Let's reunite on Plaque Day, to unveil the souvenir
And remember hazy 90's nights and friends no longer here
Our very own CBGB's

From 1990-1996, The Market Tavern in Kidderminster hosted shows by hundreds of local and international bands. Many, such as Radiohead and Carter The Unstoppable Sex Machine, went on to have huge chart success following their performances.

The venue also played a vital role in my own personal musical education.

I witnessed so many great gigs at The Tavern, including Red Kross, Carter, Frank Sidebottom, God Machine, Family Cat, The Telescopes, Top and The Primitives.

I also cut my musical teeth there, taking to the stage as a member of the bands Smedley, Farter - The Unstoppable Bowel Movement, Jackpot and Swagger.

At the end of 2020, a fantastic book by Mark Badgeman (former Tavern promoter) and Andrew Wolfman was published, superbly documenting the times and creating a renewed interest in the venue's history and achievements.

Fast forward to 2022 and, following a campaign led by Rich Morley from the band Pale Kings, a Blue Plaque was erected at the site of the old venue.

This is the song I wrote especially to perform at the unveiling.

the humdrum express

Festival at Home
artwork by
Sue Thompson

Festival At Home

the humdrum express

Copy Cats
cover stars
Elaine Lawson &
Lou Bennett

Copy Cats

the humdrum express

```
B U L C G N I M M I W S D J G
P S A L A N S M I T H N M M J
L N T R I B U T E B A N D Q T
E E T W M Q B C M F I I V B S
U D E A L O U X Y A A X X I G
G F B S Y A U D I O B O O K S
A X C H U B B Y B R O W N H H
E Z O O T J S T Y L E T I P S
L N A S A L M O N O T O N E Q
Y Y D P B N E B A Y X K D M E
A L A T E R W I T H J O O L S
D H P J J E E H F H T Y M G I
N C Y B E R H U G X X B D J B
U I N S O M N I A A G A P A W
S H C R A E S D R O W V H S Q
```

Double Edged Swords

Message Board Hooligan

A 55 year old man, with too much time on his hands
Think he must have retired too early, I can't quite understand...
Spends so much time in cyber places
On each thread leaves smiley faces
Is that what he spent years looking forward to?

You can trust me on this, because I'm in the know
My mate at the training ground passed on the info
The latest slating for ageing defenders
In-jokes, sub-plots and agendas
I'm only here for the dodgy rumours

If it's not half term, where did that come from?
I've just been threatened with the CAPS LOCK on
No ordinary supporter, he's a fanatic
41, still living in his Mum and Dad's attic
I bet he calls the phone-ins when he's not on-line!

Message Board Hooligan
He's gonna bore 'um on the forum!

This song has led something of a charmed life!

Originally released on The New Dr Who EP, it was then re-recorded for the Elevation of Trivia album in 2010.

A few years later when we put the full band together, it became a favourite to play live and eventually ended up having yet another re-record for Ultracrepidarian Soup.

I also re-use tea bags!

Lookalike Bond

Not one to stand out from the crowd, an average man on the street
I have to work long hours, still can't seem to make ends meet
People have always said I resemble an actor on TV
I don't quite know how I ended up joining a look-alike agency

The work was steady, with the opening of a sports shop and a bar
Hardly an insight into what it must be like to be a star
Until one morning, I awoke to find an unexpected twist
My double was named as the next James Bond and overnight became 'A' list

My name's Bond
They say dead ringer
My name's Bond
You only live twice, Goldfinger
My name's Bond…
James lookalike Bond

I forged signatures in Cannes; when I was there to see the sights
Seemed a far cry from switching on village Christmas lights
Factory hours, now even more a distant memory
Former workmates, I hear, are passing comment jealously

My name's Bond
I'm so well dressed, exuding charm
My name's Bond
With a wannabe Honor Blackman on my arm
My name's Bond…
James lookalike Bond

I turned on the TV news, left me shaken not stirred
As the (money) penny dropped, my whole world crashed by what I heard
My doppelganger is not all he's cracked up to be
I'll admit... It scared the living daylights out of me

His list of crime seems endless, he's facing 007 years inside
The press are out to get him, my high life's on the slide
The public are alleging other serious matters
I think I'll have to sue – my career's in tatters!

My name's Bond
Though the novelty's wearing thin
My name's Bond
At the mercy of my famous twin
My name's Bond...
James Look-alike Bond

I was tempted by the taste of celebrity and wealth
Fooled into thinking I'd be bettering myself
One small crumb of comfort to ease my loss of earning
Is the hangers on have gone; and I doubt they'll be returning
Fame based on looks, I won't be such a fool again
But I felt I needed something to help to ease the pain
I sought medical advice in a bid to ease my woe
My GP said, "Sit down, Bond"
I said, "Dr, NO!"

I'm not Bond
Forget the man I used to be
I'm not Bond
It must be someone else who looks like me

I once got mistaken for one of The Proclaimers, whilst on holiday in Greece.

I'm (partly) ashamed to admit that I signed autographs and posed for photos with adoring fans!

I didn't mean to, it just seemed like the easiest way to put an end to the embarrassing scene. I almost wished I hadn't bothered when I heard them say, "He's not as good looking in real life!"

Lookalike Bond is the tale of a professional lookalike, whose fortunes are determined by the star they pretend to be.

I love this video. Filmed at Wolverley Social Club, featuring a guest appearance from Simon Cowell!

Pop Culture Musings

Before I wander off to check how many times the word sardonic
has been used in album reviews, here are some popular culture
musings...

I'm just trying to find a sense of purpose and relevance
And rid myself of the uneasiness I feel
When I hear of established bands releasing a self titled album
That isn't their debut

People say there's no money to be made in music these days
But I'm doing OK
I've been taking bets on how many people hear a track on the
radio
And think...
"I wouldn't mind drinking warm Budweiser from a plastic bottle
whilst watching this group play an arena."
It turns out, there are thousands.
It's just one of the reasons why I've never really bothered getting
too big
I just couldn't put you through it!
And I just know they'd all clap along to Double Edged Swords
With serious timing issues

I can't help but ponder the most trivial of matters
Whilst mourning the lost art of listening.
I worry about re-integrating bass players back into musical
society
When the trend for guitar and drum duos finally dies a death
Although, I originally wrote that line eight years ago

I find myself stuck in A&E
Behind a bloke who's been injured by a feather cut at a Paul
Weller gig.
Arriving by bus, I overheard...
"I like Bob Marley, but he was a bit of a bighead calling his album
Legend"

Maybe I'm just too harsh; we've all got gaps in our knowledge.
Sandstorm / Darude... I admit, I've never been 100% sure which
was the title or artist
Perhaps I should have chosen Martial Arts over Marshall Amps?
It probably wouldn't have been as much fun
But at least I'd be able to handle myself in a fight

They say that the internet encourages inadequacy and jealousy.
I once read a story about a fellow singer/songwriter
He was so desperate for reassurance that he faked his own death
To read the outpouring of love on social media

He sadly overlooked the fact that it can be such a poisonous place
And failed to find the response he'd hoped for
His final, fragile song faded
Without applause

What a Time to Be Alive!

I must amend my CV, the current one won't impress
Was a part-time attendee at Curmudgeons R US on a YTS
I enrolled as a mature student, in desperate times
Turned up late for calligraphy classes
In the hope of being given lines
You can have that one in writing!

What a time to be alive!
I'll probably have to work till I'm 85

My circle of friends are getting older, time's flying by
From crowd to silver surfers in the blink of an eye
I try to keep my outlook youthful, but fret about my health
Trod on a snail in my vegan Doc Martens
Accidentally offended myself
Another all too often 'one of those days'

What a time to be alive!
I'll probably have to work till I'm 85

I'm scouring applications for a job that won't exist
I resumed work on my résumé; put my key skills in a list
Kitchen multi-tasking took me a while to learn
Dancing and feeding babies while tweeting Lauren Laverne
You may have heard my daily shout outs

What a time to be alive!
I'll probably have to work till I'm 85

Have a sarcastic air punch

What a Time to Be Alive was written a couple of weeks before the release of Ultracrepidarian Soup.

We kicked off the album launch set with it, at Claptrap the Venue in Stourbridge.
It was up-tempo, it felt fresh and we thought it would be an opener that would hint at the new material we'd been working on.

The date was 31st January 2020, the day before the announcement of the death of inspirational guitarist, Andy Gill.
He'd died after suffering from a 'mystery respiratory illness' after returning from a Gang Of Four tour in China.

As the mystery respiratory illnesses spread quickly across the globe, little did we know that it would be 19 months until the Humdrum full band performed to an audience again.

The return marked the end of the original line-up, with Rich Payne and Curtis Fudge replacing the departing Chris Taylor-Ashcroft and Ted Cartwright.

The Institute, Birmingham 16/09/2022
Supporting Half Man Half Biscuit

Copy Cats

They've got matching tops, they're hand in hand
The Ramones are their favourite t-shirt brand
Buy one, get one free in Matalan
Thinking for yourself never went to plan
High street steady survivor
More Betty, than Swervedriver

I read a Jamie Oliver's Feastival review
Where ex-Top Gear presenters jumped the queue
To a sign publicising ageing sleaze
It was Alex James's aptly named new cheese
Alt-Fest soon, I'll hope for gloomy weather
So we can all be alternative together

A ship called Plagiarism, fully booked, and set to sail
Bears no shame whatsoever as copy cats prevail
Ignore the progress blueprint, it's still under review
I love the way you're different
Can I be different too?

Covers gigs in pubs should be banned
If played with the aid of a music stand
I'll make no apologies for my stern stance
If you can't learn them in advance

They like to build new shops round by me
Disregarding architectural history
Ignoring all the empty ones we've got
They paved Paradise Balti and put up a parking lot
They promise outlets many towns would kill for
Like the one's people go to Merry Hill for
(Like everywhere else)

A ship called Plagiarism, fully booked, and set to sail
Bears no shame whatsoever as copy cats prevail
Ignore the progress blueprint, it's still under review
I love the way you're different
Can I be different too?

Filmed just a few months after Double Edged Swords and released in January 2016, Copy Cats was the first Humdrum Express video to feature our now established and much loved film extras.

Similar to the Carry On film cast (no, they're not all dead!), some of our stars have appeared in the majority of videos, with others making a single fleeting cameo.

I can't stress enough how much I appreciate the involvement of every single person who has given up their valuable time to join in the fun.

I suppose it also highlights just how little there is to do in Kidderminster on a Sunday!

Set in the town centre, Copy Cats is a fine blend of cat whiskers, mobility scooters and Matalan purchased Ramones t-shirts!

Coffin Cam

Coffin cam
Have you considered a coffin cam?
So your cyber fan
Can watch you decompose
The one who knows about your make-up, hair and clothes
Where you like to go and what you've cooked for tea

Time flies by for a social media butterfly
The evergreen, publicity machine

Coffin cam
Have you considered a coffin cam?
So your cyber fan
Can watch you decompose
You've joined a gym, been for a swim
On the way home, on a whim, bought an ice cream

Flutter-by, social media butterfly
The trivial, publicity machine

Is a coffin cam a good idea?
Is a coffin cam a good idea?
Is a coffin cam a good idea?
Remains to be seen

This was once described in a review as a ninety second meander to a very old joke.

I'm definitely having that!

E-Petition!

Please note that the filming of tonight's gig on smart-phones will be ridiculed by the performer...

It has been said, more than once, that I've got low aspirations
But I've just never been interested in an early morning scurry for a train whilst carrying a coffee holder
Or being the bloke with a club card on his key ring and a trolley token in his Roy Cropper style wallet
Or the man who wears shorts for 10 months of the year and then dons a wetsuit to have a paddle

Whenever I'm near the coast, I spend time wondering why you'll always find someone vacuuming in a seaside arcade
Which takes my mind off the perplexing rise of the "half and half" football scarf wearer
I guess, in many ways, I'm just a free spirit
And if anyone happens to be in any doubt, I've got the Stonehenge solstice selfies to prove it

Don't stop me I'm on a mission
Gonna start an e-petition!

Welcome to the great streaming debate where those who claim, "If I like something, I buy it," appear to be drowning out the musicians hoping to air their 0.003 penneth
I don't know about you, but I've given up on eating out these days
It's not just the expense, I can't face being told to "*enjoy*" as my order's delivered to the table.
I collected a parcel from the sorting office last week and was given the same cringe worthy command
He wasn't to know it was a home dentistry kit, but that's exactly my point
To make matters worse, I returned home to find my hurried parking had been photographed and posted on a local busybody's social media group...
Named, shamed, and hung out to dry

Don't stop me I'm on a mission
Gonna start an e-petition!

Share your troubles they say...
But I'm not ready to reveal details of the time I got run over by a
smart car whilst ironically sporting a Kylie and Jason top on
'Wear Your Old Band T-shirt To Work Day'
These are difficult enough times as it is
I sold a guitar on eBay recently
No feedback from the buyer, but then, it was only an acoustic!

Don't stop me I'm on a mission
Gonna start an e-petition!

For a Humdrum video, this was BIG budget!

FIVE "Zombies Wanted" posters were printed!
THREE face painters were hired!

*It has almost become expected that I provide a plentiful supply of Bombay
Mix for the video extras, as a generous payment for their time and
commitment to the cause!*

*On this occasion, I also added complimentary cookies, cakes and crisps to
the nourishing nibbles menu, all lavishly laid on to entice some "extra
extras" to the scene in Stourbridge.*

We didn't need a script for this one!
*As our horrifying horde of zombies emerged from our High Street hideout
at Claptrap the Venue, the Sunday shoppers were shocked, passers-by
perplexed and town-centre traffic brought to a standstill.*

*The Stourbridge News held the front page and NJT Media miraculously
pulled out all the stops to complete the editing in time for a Halloween
release.*

E-Petition!

Nick J Townsend (left)
Humdrum video genius

If Only I'd Watched Blue Peter

I can't keep up with the Joneses, one-upmanship always has a catch
My neighbour's had a wet room fitted but all I've got's a damp patch
Wheelie bin decals, well they look so smart
I'm not sure what you intended but they certainly set you apart

Forty-something blokes with wide eyes, perusing toy shop shelves
For the latest Star Wars figures to buy for themselves
You know they'll never be opened, but kept in their box
While kids are left disappointed when the stores are low on stocks

Spiritual hopefuls practice meditation techniques
And purchase healing crystals from seaside boutiques
We all look for something on which to place our hopes
Born on the cusp I've got no faith in horoscopes

Empowering slogans to give yourself a boost
My tee-shirt says that "I'm unique" but it's probably mass produced

The clothing ads in Sunday mags aren't quite to my taste
Not the type of guy who'd multi-buy an elasticated waist
You got a 92 piece dining set in a shopping channel deal
When you're home alone in front of the TV to eat each meal

I grew up watching Telly Savalas and other American cops
Now I'm on telly surveillance, caught pinching lollipops
The punishment seems, hefty I know it's not right to steal
If only I'd watched Blue Peter, I might know how to appeal

*Dedicated to my good friend Jase (The Ace) Kernohan, who loves
a bit of whimsy!*

Chipsticks

The supermarket plays out a muzak re-write
Of Toploader's 'Dancing in the Moonlight'

A fella at checkout starts to sing-along
I try to blot it out but the feeling's too strong
I run for the door without paying for my multi-pack
Of chipsticks

For an older guy, I was pretty quick off the blocks
Till I was wrestled to the ground by bloke in joggers and Crocs

I lay there surrounded, pleading my defence
Upended by a man with a chronic fashion sense
This double embarrassment wasn't how I'd planned my day

Assumptions were made about my finances
No knowledge of the mitigating circumstances

Sympathy was sadly lacking for my plight
The have-a-go hero sang 'Basking in the Limelight'

He'd made a name for himself and milked the applause
How could he have known Toploader were the cause?
The fact that he liked them came as no surprise

The store manager was an unforgiving man
Issued me with a stern look and a lifetime ban

The police rocked up for my maize-based crime
They said they'd take the swag as it was nearly lunchtime
Guess what was playing in their car as they drove away...

The original full band line-up:
Chris Taylor-Ashcroft, Ian Passey,
Carl Bayliss, Andrew Boswell.
It was soon to be enhanced
by the sax-iness of Ted Cartwright

2021 - 2022
Rich Payne, Carl Bayliss, Ian Passey,
Andrew Boswell, Curtis Fudge

Secret Troll

He's an art loving, Bach listening, rugby supporting,
Choir singing, wine drinking, beige chino sporting
Steam fair attending, antique shop browsing
Responsible guy, works in social housing

Cheese Club monthly membership renewed
Takes an early morning dip in the lake at Latitude
A self proclaimed expert on Serbian street food
Now the time has come to let the cat out the bag...

Secret troll
He's a secret troll
A secret troll, thrives on control
And it seems his daily goal
Is trolling me

A local listed building puts on an ice cream fair
Once his sculpture class is over, he'll be there
He likes a public cause to which he loudly can donate
His affable persona hides a snidely trait

A needle crafter who seems needled by me
And I've become the subject, of his toxicity
Piping up to put me down at every opportunity
Now the time has come... to turn the tide

Secret troll
He's a secret troll
A secret troll, thrives on control
And it seems his daily goal
Is trolling me

He likes to raise a glass to toast English wine week
Doesn't spread much cheer with his online vicious streak
I've looked him up, he doesn't use a pseudonym
I'm embarrassed to be trolled by a bloke as wet as him

Admiring a steam roller at a vintage show
I saw him take the opportunity for a photo
Apparently the handbrake slipped and he was squashed below
Flattening him into the past tense (please believe it was coincidence!)

Secret troll
He was a secret troll
A secret troll, thrived on control
And it seemed his daily goal
Was trolling me

Secret troll
He was a secret troll
A secret troll, thrived on control
Now he's buried in a hole…
No longer trolling me!

Radio legend, 'Whispering' Bob Harris has publicly stated on a couple of occasions that The Humdrum Express is the best band name EVER!

The second time he mentioned it was on Twitter where, unsurprisingly, someone replied with, "No it isn't, it's the worst."

I couldn't resist looking up the person responsible for the unnecessary unkindness. . His biog read… "Art loving, wine drinking, steam fair attending, music fan"

The rest, as they say….

Catch A Fallen Star...

Work has all but dried up for me
I was a TV game show host in the '70s.
Too long out the limelight, no-one wants to know
12 million viewers once enjoyed the show, back then
Even past their sell by date entertainers have to eat
And my every day tasks are laughed at in the street

There's a daily record of my fall from grace
As school kids hold their phones up to my face
How I regret adopting that dire catchphrase
But we all had to have one back in those days
From golden haired sitcom boy about town
To grey whiskered man in a dressing gown

As I dozed in my chair, heard a knock too loud to ignore
Two stern face boys in blue at my front door
Must join them at the station, things to explain
I'm asked to take a trip down Yew Tree Lane
As I'm handcuffed in the back of the car
They joke about catching a fallen star

Even though there are no charges, I'm branded a liar
Not guilty is seen as, "no smoke without fire"

I'd built up a fading memory of fame
Twilight years with mud stuck my name
No longer a harmless joke to passers by
There's a hateful tone as insults fly
Anonymous complaints, public accusations
Hands are rubbed in anticipation
Quenching their thirst, granting their wish
While taking the heat off the bigger fish

Waiting for the next name

Online
Beer Club

Online Beer Club

He says mainstream ales, just bore him
The man who's got it all, but needs someone to make decisions for
him
I know you've got the facts, and who am I to doubt it
"Beer tastes better when you know a bit more about it"
Apparently

The choice is never ending
For the connoisseur or the condescending
From the online club!

Spring-like hops with a yeasty bite
The recipe for working up an appetite
Although he quite fancied a bag of chips
Opted for artisan kale and ricotta dips
See instagram for proof

Watch my love of life diminish
When I hear of peach aromas and a zingy grapefruit finish
From the online club!

A misconstrued complexity
Craving authenticity
An elusive, bitter quality
Not sure if that's the drinkers or the ales

He loves to recall the first time he said
He was off to work on his crafts, in his shed
His palate's cleansed with his selection
Drinking alone with his vinyl collection
Hipster paradise

Pumpkin gluten-free's my favourite
It's not just millennials who savour it
I've joined the online club!

A misconstrued complexity
Craving authenticity
An elusive, bitter quality
Not sure if that's the drinkers or the ales

The choice is never ending
For the connoisseur or the condescending
From the online club!

You don't hear much about hipsters anymore.
Maybe Covid killed them off?
Maybe drinking craft ale from cracked teapot just became too common!

The filming for the Online Beer Club video, once again, proved to be eventful...

On the day of the shoot, I arrived at Kidderminster Hospital (already fully bandaged) for the opening scene.

I can't remember if I was early or Nick J Townsend was running late, but I do recall sweating profusely in the car, too scared to get out until he arrived!

The next stop was Paul Smith's man cave in Bewdley. Driving there was something of an experience with slipping bandages hampering my vision. The return journey was memorable too - being chased around the Kidderminster ring road by a gang of youths, who were obviously too young to remember The Invisible Man!

I'll never forget the sense of joy and relief as I walked into The King & Castle to be greeted by our welcoming horde of video 'hipsters' - no doubt buoyed by the prospect of being able to drink beer on-set!

One of the hottest and most enjoyable days of the summer, captured forever.

"Woo hoo!"

The Day My Career Died

Some things are made for each other
Some things need love and time to grow
Some things, I'm bored of seeing together
Like Comedy. Panel. And Show

When I was young I'd dream of being a Luddite
Although aware it was a dying trade
My views on technology embracing
Led to some lengthy spells unpaid

Why can't these things happen to you?

Dangling the carrot, taking the bait, happened to coincide
My sledgehammer stolen in a cruel twist of fate
The day my career died

An evening of cheap wine and facebook
Makes for a sore head and regrets
Think of it as all good preparation
For the night when you mix scotch with on-line bets

Why can't these things happen to you?

Dangling the carrot, taking the bait, happened to coincide
My sledgehammer stolen in a cruel twist of fate
The day my career died

Lacking in support, I was surprised
By revelations smashed to smithereens
"Be a forward thinker" I was advised
I must find time to find out what it means

Headline writers found it hard to resist
As they queued up to report on my descent
According to the story's final twist
I was loitering without intent

Why can't these things happen to you?

Dangling the carrot, taking the bait, happened to coincide
My sledgehammer stolen in a cruel twist of fate
The day my career died!

Keepin' Score

To atone for my errors
I'd kill the man for all seasons
Haven't planned how I'd do it
Or thought through my reasons

I could fill your head with images of sunny days
But I'll leave it to the others to bring out the clichés

There's a battle commencing
Outside your door
The helpless vs. the hopeless
Should be close, I'm keeping score!

It's in the papers
Search for a saviour
Under the headline
'Who's NOT resigned to failure?'

There's no word on television, no on-screen rapport
You don't watch and I won't watch, no-one's watching anymore

There's a battle commencing
Outside your door
The helpless vs. the hopeless
Should be close, I'm keeping score!

I want my money back; I'd paid for the surprise
The elevation of trivia is more than just disguise

Tuesday morning drizzle
Comfort for downhearted
Busy doing something
You wished you'd never started

Old fashioned endearment, I know you can't resist
Consult your doctor, if symptoms persist!

There's a battle commencing
We've seen these teams before
The helpless vs. the hopeless
Should be close, I'm keeping score!

Worcester Music Festival
2022 at The Firefly

Photographs by
Peter Williams (left)
and Cerys John (below)

When Peter Shilton Tweets…

Often used, by the TV news
Wheeled out to share Nationalistic views, on repeat
Tapping on his phone, while sitting on the throne
You can almost hear a collective groan
When Peter Shilton Tweets

In '86, indecisive
These days, divisive
The hand of God Save the Queen

Those who mock, feel the force of a timely block
We could have done with one at Wembley in '73
He marshals his defence by pretending to take offence
And when it looks like turning ugly he calls up Beardsley!

*During the first lockdown, I lost a great deal of interest in song writing.
Without gigs to focus on, or rehearsals and events to plan, I just
couldn't get into the groove.*

*When the sequel (Lockdown 2) arrived, I was determined to make up for
lost time. We'd had a taste of freedom, albeit socially distanced, but
the general feeling was far more positive for the future.*

*It was actually another football song that kick-started my 'return to form'.
I had the idea for Denim In The Dugout after watching Barnsley manager,
Gerhard Struber, celebrating his team's last gasp Championship survival
by running down the touchline, sporting grey skinny jeans!*

*One Man's Tat, Christmas With Evan Dando and When Peter Shilton
Tweets were all written shortly afterwards, sowing the seeds for the
Forward Defensive album*

*Why am I telling you this?
Because this is by far the shortest lyric in the book and it's a
handy way of filling page space!*

Third Choice Keeper

I'm a third choice keeper, rarely called upon
There's great camaraderie in the goalie's union
I'm a third choice keeper, earn a fair amount
Paid each month into my non-savers account

My best performances are witnessed at training grounds
You may have seen me on the bench in the league cup early rounds
I hate coaches' calls to play out from the back
And the shouts to put my crisps down when facing a counter attack

I'm a third choice keeper, rarely called upon
There's great camaraderie in the goalie's union
I'm a third choice keeper, earn a fair amount
Paid each month into my non-savers account

45 appearances, spanning 20 years
I played 6 times one season, the most in my career
Winner's medals adorn my walls without playing a game
On each year's team photo I'm the one that you can't name

The understudy's understudy; unsung, unique
I rarely work on Saturdays but train hard in the week
I dream of saving penalties in a shoot out in the cup
But I'm here to make the number of home-grown players up

I'm a third choice keeper, rarely called upon
There's great camaraderie in the goalie's union
I'm a third choice keeper, earn a fair amount
Paid each month into my non-savers account

Fading Stars on Social Media

Talking in the pub about singers
Whose careers took a sharp nose-dive
One name caused more debate than most
As to whether he was dead or still alive
After much deliberation
I looked him up on Wikipedia
Who confirmed that he was still with us, but warned
Avoid on social media!

I couldn't resist the temptation,
Added him as a friend
He accepted within seconds
And then proceeded to send
A string of generic messages
To thank me for being his "fan"
And a list of future tour dates saying
"Get to as many as you can"

Then he liked and shared my old posts
Although nice, it aroused concern
When he sent me one more message to say
He hoped I'd do the same in return
I assumed this constant barrage
Would soon ease off in time
When (ding!)
"I've shared 30 of yours; you've only shared 6 of mine"

He's desperate for attention
Spouting controversial views
Just to spark reaction
With his take on the day's news
His opinion can't be faulted
Nor his petulant behaviour
Re-writing musical history
To spin it in his favour

I felt sorry for him more than anything
It seemed so easy to mock him
Until Coldplay were named as his favourite band
Then I knew it was time to block him!
In a cyber world of needy
You'll find they're even needier
A word of advice, avoid if you can
Fading stars on social media!

This is a completely fictional piece, although I'm often asked who inspired it.

I'm saying nothing, especially about The Icicle Works...

Wed 30th Jan
Playing live on Steve Lamacq's
BBC Radio 6 Music show

4 -7pm
Independent Venue Week

What a Carry On!

The big mouth, small-mind brigade are in force again
Although that probably implies that they've been away
Give off a whiff of arrogance to hide their failings
As I walked past, I was exhaling
That rare piece of good news made my day

Safe in the knowledge that sometime they'll fall
What an insight! What a carry on!
Can I pay to be a fly on the wall?
What an insight! What a carry on!

Can't meet half way on this, I'm running late
The promise of a sympathetic ear, with no set date
You don't have to tell me, I know what you're thinking
It's the age of choice, yet my options are shrinking
There's no prize for punching above your weight

Safe in the knowledge that sometime they'll fall
What an insight! What a carry on!
Can I pay to be a fly on the wall?
What an insight! What a carry on!
The stolen file read, "Toe the line"
Now it's cards on the table time

Nostalgia of poor quality; packaged up, processed as cheese
So much for the thrill of discovery
Searching for ideas down the market, sweep new hope under
the carpet
The shop choice is pound or charity

Safe in the knowledge that sometime they'll fall
What an insight! What a carry on!
Can I pay to be a fly on the wall?
What an insight! What a carry on!
The stolen file read, "Toe the line"
Now it's cards on the table time

My Top Five...
Carry On Films:

Abroad
Cabby
Camping
At Your Convenience
Again Doctor

Cynical Thrill Seeker

Don't waste time trying to work out how many fitness fanatics
Shane McGowan's outliving...
Accept it as one life's more enjoyable quirks
The baffling popularity of operatic stadium fillers Muse is,
however, a different matter entirely
One that will continue costing me hours of valuable sleep

When going to watch professional football, extra care should be
taken to ensure you don't arrive early enough to endure pre-
match entertainment
Fifty odd school kids performing a dance routine to "Mickey" by
Toni Basil should play no part in any sporting fixture

I've nothing but sympathy for the supermarket workers, who are
now forced to ask customers if they'd like help packing more than
two items
I appreciate it's far worse for them than me, but there is a reason
why I haven't asked for phone top up, stamps, lottery or scratch
cards

I don't think I'll ever understand the concept of chill-out music
Surely records should excite, enlighten, galvanise, amuse or
inspire?
We seem to be wasting each others time.
Why not turn off, relax and enjoy rare silence?

Is there anything more excruciating than a so called festival
band?
Always with too many people on stage, changing instruments
between songs
Each democratic half baked idea lasts twelve minutes...
Longer than it needs to

Why not consider taking up an interesting new hobby?
I've recently started posting false information on DIY forums
It's easy to mask my lack of knowledge with false bravado
And the on-line fury that follows
Is addictively entertaining!

A new national rich list has been published, dissected and
discussed at length by TV experts
While my own omission came as little surprise, I was amazed to
see there was no place for the man who makes suits for stand up
comedians
The strange breed who spend their evenings talking about
themselves for two hours at a time to a roomful of strangers
All seem to either suffer from a sudden creative by pass or choose
not to take up on the opportunity to wear what they want to work

Can excuses honestly be made for pub quiz cheats, nasal
newsreaders and do-gooders who give up alcohol for the whole of
January?
Copy and paste philosophers, ground floor gaffers and small
groups of men who tinker with engines on their rare days off work
Heels are kicked in draughty industrial units, brains wracked in
a desperate hope of finding a new form of non-organized escape
Trying times for your average cynical thrill seeker

These, are trying times

Photographs by Andy Miles

2019 at Claptrap the Venue, Stourbridge

2020 Tuning up - A rare sight!

You'll Always Find Me in the Kitchen at Watch Parties

A mate of mine, known locally as the singing chef
Thought he'd spend some of his furlough time on his musical
hobby
And set about cooking up a plan to stream his first ever live
acoustic gig

He spent a day preparing for the online extravaganza
Half an hour running through the set
Ten minutes perfecting his "lean-in switch off technique"
which would follow the final track
And six hours painting a huge 'PayPal Me' sign

He always was a romantic daydreamer
And thought the performance might help to top up his reduced
wages
And maybe re-connect with those he was missing
But, most of all, take his mind off his employment uncertainty

You'll always find him in the kitchen at watch parties

Event page shared, camera strategically placed
He'd even borrowed a spotlight in the hope that his sign could be
seen more clearly.
I felt slightly nervous for him, but there was no going back
It was time, at last, to go live

It all started so well.
It was noted that there were 30 people watching
The biggest crowd he'd played to in years!
As he openly admitted, the lack of applause at the end of each
song
Was something he was already well accustomed to

You'll always find him in the kitchen at watch parties

His natural warmth and humility made up for the occasional lack of finesse
I couldn't help but feel a sense of pride at seeing a mate do well
The likes and comments soon started to fly in
And curiosity found me scrolling through

It would appear that most seemed to mention, and discuss
Not the so much the music but a row of garish underpants left airing in full view on the radiator
Note to self, never do a home gig on wash day

You'll always find him in the kitchen at watch parties

Knowing him to be a sensitive soul
I was worried he might take the comments to heart
Especially having spent a lot of time on his own recently

I think I'll drop him a message, just to check that he's ok
You should always look after those furloughed friends

Maybe I could offer him some advice by saying, "Time is a great healer"
It's a cliché I know, but he might be consoled by me telling him
"He'll stream again, don't know where, don't know when
But I know he'll stream again"

Roll Out the Red Carpet

Often seen in the local press under the headline "next big thing"
Fame chasing delusion, from those who love to sing
Household names... next year, they hope
This week they're booked for weddings, gigs and the opening of
an envelope

She said she's quite well known round our way
The postman asked for her autograph just the other day
He said "please sign here - sorry to intrude"
Then he gave her a parcel, to show his gratitude

Roll out the red carpet - Hail the next big thing
From a mention in the gig guide to a full review
In the absence of their name in lights
Their face in print will do

He returns to play in the town, on a break from his workload
Failing to mention he's still living down the road
Talks loudly of the glamour and the glitz
And not the evenings spent at home, alone, self adding
You Tube hits

You'd think trainee celebrities might go around disguised
Instead of shopping in their stage wear in the hope they're
recognised
The only time that they prefer to hide
Is when they're buying extra copies of each paper they're inside

Roll out the red carpet - Hail the next big thing
From a mention in the gig guide to a full review
In the absence of their name in lights
Their face in print will do

Last week's edition was labelled a disgrace
Some new local band had taken up his column space
He said, "They've not got my talent or support"
Then takes time to remind us that he's not the jealous sort!

The Rose Theatre, Kidderminster 07/10/2017
An evening with The Humdrum Express

Nostalgia for Beginners

Sitting at the front of a double decker
A carved wooden bookend in the shape of a woodpecker
Scooby Doo, Mystery Machine
League Ladders in Shoot! Magazine
Saturday evenings waiting in the rain
The Sports Argus driver's late again
Spot the Ball, Spud-U-Like
Builder's bum, park your bike

We're still drawn in the cup - Against the team
We're due to play - The same week in the league

Berni Inn, Crossroads motel
Azumah Nelson, Pat Cowdell
New Romantics, New Wave
One Step Beyond, One Foot in the Grave

We're still drawn in the cup - Against the team
We're due to play - The same week in the league

How can this happen? I hear you say
One draws the home team, another draws away
A challenging outcome, a challenging cup
Year on year this quirk crops up

Bubble gum cards, Panini stickers
Opal Fruits, Starburst, Marathon, Snickers
Amos Brearly, Woolpack
Shoestring, Bergerac
We're With The Woolwich, Streetband – Toast!
Ronnie Radford, Rentaghost
33 1/3
3310
Kicking off at 3pm

We're still drawn in the cup
Against the team
We're due to play
The same week in the league

Leopard Print Onesie

Stuck scriptwriters pen the return of an old soap rogue
In a desperate bid to revive interest and boost ratings
It's FA Cup weekend... When stand in pundits criticise managers
For fielding reserves
Join us tonight at 9, as we take a nostalgic look back
To when times were similarly poor
But the music was much better...
Bertrand Russell, Isaac Newton, Pythagoras, Einstein
Joey Barton

Inspiring the next generation...

Radio callers gloat about listening to the show everyday
Whilst working from home
And at last, I understand why tradesmen on building sites
Never bother to quite tune them in properly
Yet another long distance lorry driver pulls into a lay-by in tears
To text in, upon hearing an emotional song
A discussion on crisp pack sell-by dates
Interspersed with old kids TV themes

Inspiring the next generation...

The revival of something not much good in the first place
Gathers momentum
While original mods attach mirrors to mobility scooters
I can't help but worry about whether
The mods, skins and rude boys of tomorrow
Will dress in Andy Murray polo shirts
Singer/songwriters' collaboration threats
Having reached retrospective points in their careers
Self promotion reminiscent, of wind-chimes in a hurricane

Inspiring the next generation...

Sport can still unite as I'm sure it will forever
'Cause when things don't go your way, it's nice to boo together

Considering it's the age of the conspiracy theory…
I'm surprised no-one's questioned
How the fella off The Apprentice got the Countdown job
Of course, I'm all for re-cycling, but I just reckon bags for life
Should become cheaper as you get older
The decline of social drinking, replaced by the more affordable
Junk food escape route
Deep Pan's People, Greggs & Co!
The Gastric Band are this weeks Top of the Ops

Inspiring the next generation…

A scuffle breaks out in the record store day queue
Highlighting the competitive pursuit of vinyl rarities
My time's often spent trying to get my head round the fact
That Sam Smith sells more records than TV Smith
I'm at least temporarily buoyed by the imminent arrival
Of +2 channels and bird flu
Nom nom, bake off, hit me with your selfie stick
Leopard print onesie!

Inspiring the next generation…

*I can't stress enough, how much Steve Lamacq's support means to me.
Not only has he helped shape my music tastes over the years, his BBC6
Music shows have been a daily source of entertainment and a vital tool in
my discovery of new bands to fall in love with.*

*Following the first plays of Festival at Home, Steve has pretty much
played every Humdrum Express release since. I've never had
management or a radio plugger; I've simply sent him the tracks with a
polite note, thanking him for the previous airplay.*

When you consider, after play-listed tracks, the limited scope each DJ has to choose songs for their own shows, it's incredibly humbling to have received as much airtime as I have.

At the beginning of 2019, it was announced that Lammo would be bringing his show to Worcester as part of Independent Venue Week, when he tours the country visiting grass roots music venues.

I had desperately hoped to be included in the line up at The Marr's Bar, which Steve would attend after his live broadcast but, sadly, it wasn't to be.
The venue had chosen their acts for the night and I wasn't going to be part of it.

A couple of weeks ahead of his visit, I received an email from Steve asking if I'd mind popping over to Worcester to perform two songs and have a chat live on his show!
I couldn't believe it!

The programme was aired from the studios at BBC Hereford & Worcester where, on Wednesday 30th January, I played a brand new song (Motivational Wall Art) and a slightly altered version of Leopard Print Onesie.
Below is the extra verse that was written for the show, with a nod to Indie Venue Week and some of the great venues we've lost over the years…

In recent years, developers have moved in next to pre-existing music venues, built apartments and sold them to those who like complaining
Don't buy flats, buy into the importance of history
Because the best gigs can happen in the smallest rooms
Where creativity and diverse community provide a stage for emerging acts
Let's not forget the great ones we've already lost…

The Cockpit
The Metro
The Boardwalk
Market Tavern and
The Square

They inspired a generation

The Curse of the Modern Musician

I really like your music and your words
But the need for praise can be misleading
It's like finding a bogey in a library book
Which only serves to put me off my reading

Musicians are guilty of the modern curse
With their need to update each time they write a verse
We'd best move fast as it may get worse
A social network habit leaves less time to rehearse

Just three pounds a month is all we're asking
To enrol them on a self-awareness plan
As tax avoiding millionaire celebrities might say
Please, general public, give us all you can

Musicians are guilty of the modern curse
With their need to update each time they write a verse
We'd best move fast as it may get worse
A social network habit leaves less time to rehearse

Song writing exertion leaves you in need of a diversion
Speak in the third person, seeking cyber reassertion

My flippant nature sometimes takes over
Got to hear this work in progress one more time
I haven't had such fun since Snow Patrol got writer's block
Astound me with your couplets; amaze me with your rhyme

Musicians are guilty of the modern curse
With their need to update each time they write a verse
We'd best move fast as it may get worse
A social network habit leaves less time to rehearse

The Batman & Robin themed video for The Curse of the Modern Musician has a genuine Gotham City feel. You'd never guess it was filmed in Stourbridge!

Mike Alma took on the role of the "Boy" Wonder and, if I remember correctly, he kept the costume afterwards, "just in case it might come in handy…"

The overriding memory of the day was the genuine goodwill and warmth shown to us by pretty much everyone we encountered.

Children and adults alike made us feel like proper superheroes!

The
Curse
Of
The
Modern
Musician

Celebrity Death Etiquette

Ah, the selfie of those crocodile tears in full flow
To show how upset you think you should appear to be
The must use hashtags... #gutted and #legend
This, after all, was your hero, remember?
Don't be disheartened if you're not first to break the news
There's always someone, somewhere who won't have heard
It may not seem like it, but time...
Time-line is a great healer

Celebrity Death, Celebrity Death Etiquette
Celebrity Death, Celebrity Death Etiquette

At last, the opportunity you've been waiting for
To scroll through those endless phone photos
To re-share that blurry image of you
Invading the freshly deceased's privacy during a chance
encounter
How long should I wait before it's OK to make a joke at their
expense?
Is a question you never thought to ask
Shrewdly turning someone's passing
Into more about you than them

Celebrity Death, Celebrity Death Etiquette
Celebrity Death, Celebrity Death Etiquette

Re-posting the announcement of someone's demise
Years after the event has occurred is… admittedly a joy
You can't fool all of the people all of the time but, in this instance
The percentage is high
eBay vultures circle, with cold hopes of cashing in on misfortune
While it remains current
One day, it will be their turn
With no bids, no watchers and no interest

Celebrity Death, Celebrity Death Etiquette
Celebrity Death, Celebrity Death Etiquette

Shrewdly turning someone's passing into more about you than
them

*I once posted news of the passing of 'Blakey' from On The Buses (actor
Stephen Lewis) long after his death.*
*My stopwatch recorded a time of 1 minute 12 seconds before someone
piped up to tell me he'd died years ago!*

Misinterpretation

Get yourself a priority ticket
All you need is the right credit card or phone contract
Who said rock n roll's dead?
A dedication, for those who spend far too much time thinking
Yet still remain, sadly, none the wiser
Uninspiring surroundings, under achievers
Unsigned band rivalry and factory floor petulance prevail
No matter what your sport of choice
I promise no badge kissing
And therefore expect no false acts of loyalty in return

Enthusiasts who've spent years fuelling their passion
Time and minds lovingly filled with rare trivia
Kicked in the teeth as they're upstaged by a smart-arse Google
expert
During a momentary memory lapse
I'm bored. Humour me!
Well, I've been described as "brilliant"
By TV and radio presenter Edith Bowman
Not strictly true but its how she refers to all other artists
So there's no reason to assume I'd be excluded.

The age of the bed sheet banner
Misspelled protest versus Un-moving tributes
See also, spacing issues
I've got my mind on my money and my money...
On a long shot, running in the 3.15 at Market Rasen
I'm doomed, and staring at the prospect of another job
That'll hinder my planned session of day dreaming
Stand by for another bout of petty parking space arguments
A sight for four eyes

I can sense an intensifying climate of injustice
But I'm told tonight looks good on the telly
Coming up, "All You Can Eat – The Gut Buster Special"
Followed by a new series of "When Hearts Attack"
Looking up to let downs can lose its appeal
Amidst the tiring repetition of the gruelling daily grind
Especially when suffering from an unconvincing overuse...

... Of the dramatic pause

Denim in the Dugout

He used to wear a suit until he axed it
Found a casual substitute - stonewashed, relaxed fit
From Brazil to Bulgaria
On the touchline and technical area
Football managers are wearing jeans

They shelved sports wear; heard ripped slim fit looked hotter
When sported by Sean Dyche and Graham Potter
An assistant coach in shorts in December
Is an image I'd rather not remember
Now football managers are wearing jeans

Brendan Rodgers often goes out shopping
The fashion league is one he dreams of topping
A recent acid-wash acquisition
Turned heads of those held back by tradition
Football managers are wearing jeans

Away fans crudely chanted "What's he got on?"
"Dark blue, distressed, snug fit hard wearing cotton"
There's outfit help for those in need
From Kenny Jacket and Neil Harris-Tweed

Neil Warnock's flares flap in the breeze
Steve Bruce cuts a dash in dungarees
No foul committed, the ref says, "Play on"
Garry Monk's transferred to spray-ons
Football managers are wearing jeans

2-0 down half time at Grimsby Town
His wardrobe and his team get a dressing down
Roy Hodgson still looks sharp in a suit, but
Wait till you see Bielsa in boot cut!

Excitement mounting on cup final day
Double denim droves down Wembley Way
A united apparel from dugout to crowd
Rossi and Parfitt would be so proud
Football managers are wearing jeans

Football managers are wearing jeans
It's a real game changer!
Football managers are wearing jeans
A tactical jean-ius!
Football managers are wearing jeans
A victory over two legs!

Ultracrepidarian Soup album launch
Claptrap the Venue, Stourbridge 31/01/2020

We were joined by special guest TV Smith for the encore,
a storming rendition of Gary Gilmore's Eyes!

Missing The Point

Is this anymore than a passing phase?
Is your only care to say, "I was there?"
No emotional ties
It's fine to observe, until they have the nerve
To assume my level of interest is the same as theirs

Fish out of water
Bluffing their way through
Conversations, oblivious to
The fact that there's no passion and you're missing the point

Do you remember the good old days?
When comic actors and stand-up comedians
Led such tortured private lives
Paint on the smile
You think your emotional depth is the same as theirs

Fish out of water
Bluffing their way through
Conversations, oblivious to
The fact that there's no passion and you're missing the point

Feel free to enthuse, I won't refuse
Facts and figures, details and dates
Give me the agonising build up
And the post-match debate

Fish out of water
Bluffing their way through
Conversations, oblivious to
The fact that there's no passion and you're missing the point

So give me...
Train spotters, secret tacticians
Vinyl junkies, cricket statisticians
Model makers, avid collectors

One Man's Tat
(Is another Man's Treasure)

I've got a signed photo of Terry and June and a tankard off
Bullseye
Got lots of yellow, green and brown snooker balls, they were a
baulk buy
I've got a recipe for beans on toast with all the trimmings
I've got the box that Brian Lara wore during his record breaking
innings

One Man's Tat is another Man's Treasure

I've got a Qualcast mower, a gold leaf blower and a
Tamagotchi pet
I've even got, ironically, an Alanis Morisette cassette
I've got newspaper cuttings from the opening of the Channel
Tunnel
I've got a life-sized cut-out... of Sally Gunnell!

One Man's Tat is another Man's Treasure

I've got every episode of The Brittas Empire on VHS
I've got a Corgi Bat Mobile and a Corby trouser press
I've got a Stella McCartney lime green leatherette Pac-A-Mac
I've got a Crackerjack pencil (CRACKERJACK!)

One Man's Tat is another Man's Treasure

I sometimes use my gig merch stand as an opportunity to get rid of a few bits of old tat that are lying around the house.

It's cheaper than paying for a car boot sale pitch and it hopefully provides a talking point and welcome change from the usual items that most bands have on offer!

Sadly, I don't own everything listed in the song, although I do have a life-sized cut-out of Sally Gunnell (who hasn't?!) and a signed photo of Terry and June (not for sale).

This one's for the hoarders!

The Assembly, Leamington Spa
17/03/2023
Supporting Half Man Half Biscuit

Fans Lost Forever

Over at the channel where football didn't exist before '92
Pretty boy ex-playing pundits stretch their vocabulary
He's a top, top, top player
He's a top, top, top player
He's a top, top... yes, we get the idea

I'm sure there was a time when Match of the Day featured the
afternoon's best game to open the show, regardless of league
position
Welcome to the lowlights, where so-called experts can't even be
bothered to learn the names of more than 3 players, from teams
outside the top 6

Their blasé indifference, a license payer's own goal
They should get over the fact that they used to play...
Before the money spiralled out of control

Mortgage free fifty-something's whose kids have grown and left
home try to fill the void - with mild enthusiasm.
Revelling in their freedom to enjoy the day out
Buy the most expensive tickets, and then talk throughout
Discussing games from the past and the shareholders' meeting

They moan that the atmosphere, these days, is not the same
I'm sure they'll still be here, long after I'm priced out the game

Weakened sides against tough opposition
Kick off times ruled by television
We're customers, our days as fans are gone
Don't put yourself through the hurt
Of a player's name printed on a shirt
In the next transfer window they'll move on

Down at grass roots level, competitive parents nurture their
lottery ticket
Eight year old robots with their flair coached out
Until they tick the boxes required by a scout
All desperate to become the next self obsessed pampered arsehole

Of course, this gets dragged up in the two weeks of outrage
When England get knocked out the World Cup at the group stage

Build up false hopes of winning and enjoy the discontent
Build 'em up to knock 'em down
All that flag-waving clouds judgement

Don't waste time on club tradition
Join the pursuit of unfair position
The quick fix era hailed from plastic seats
Restlessness to be appeased
By new investment from overseas
And a promise to take care of balance sheets

Turkey Teeth

Well, the airport décor's dated
In need of restyling
There's a sombre look from those in the queue
As if they're scared of smiling
Even early morning pre flight booze can't provide relief
As they board the flight to Istanbul to get their Turkey teeth

On a cut-price crowns charter to foreign lands
Clutching photographs of Rylan in their hands

The Tik Tok trending peer pressure
For crooked corrective cosmetics
Inspires demand for the biggest, brightest
Dental prosthetics
A Hollywood smile at a discount price
Seems like money well spent
Because a Hollywood smile is just what you need
When you live in Stoke-on-Trent!

On a cut-price crowns charter to foreign lands
Clutching photographs of Rylan in their hands

Give Us A Smile! Pearly White!
Give Us A Smile! Ultra Bright!
Give Us A Smile! Pearly White!
Give Us A Smile! Ultra Bright!

They've all booked serious over sizing
Bigger than they need
Their incisors shaved into points and
Boy, it's gonna bleed
Dining on soup for the next six weeks
Drinking through straws
They're not helping themselves if they want to lose
Their playground nickname 'Jaws'

On a cut-price crowns charter to foreign lands
Clutching photographs of Rylan in their hands

The procedure didn't go to plan
Catastrophic complications
An agonising abscess necessitates need
For root canal operations
Unbearable pain, sensitive nerves, flying home in tears
While the NHS are left to pick up the pieces
From your bargain bin veneers

On a cut-price crowns charter from foreign lands
Clutching compensation claim forms in their hands

Turkey Teeth is the first of a new batch of songs to feature the dual guitar attack of Rich Payne and 'new boy' Brendan Moran, who replaced Curtis Fudge at the end of 2022.

I saw a news item on BBC Breakfast, previewing an upcoming documentary on the rising number of people travelling to Turkey for new gnashers.

I didn't watch the full documentary later that night.
I didn't need to – the song was finished by lunchtime!

the humdrum express

little victories

Thank you so much for
buying (or borrowing) this book.

Ian Passey 2023